CRAFT ATTACK!

RECYCLING CRAFTS

Annalees Lim

Gareth Stevens
Publishing

Please visit our website, www.garethstevens.com. For a free color catalog of all our high-quality books, call toll free 1-800-542-2595 or fax 1-877-542-2596.

Library of Congress Cataloging-in-Publication Data

Lim, Annalees.
Recycling crafts / by Annalees Lim.
    pages cm. — (Craft attack)
Includes bibliographical references and index.
ISBN 978-1-4824-0220-9 (pbk.)
ISBN 978-1-4824-0221-6 (6-pack)
ISBN 978-1-4824-0218-6 (library binding)
1. Handicraft—Juvenile literature. 2. House furnishings—Juvenile literature. 3. Refuse as art material—Juvenile literature. 4. Recycled products—Juvenile literature. I. Title.
TT160.L4853 2014
745.5—dc23

2013021483

First Edition

Published in 2014 by
Gareth Stevens Publishing
111 East 14th Street, Suite 349
New York, NY 10003

Editors: Joe Harris and Sara Gerlings
Design: Elaine Wilkinson
Cover design: Elaine Wilkinson
Photography: Simon Pask

Printed in the United States of America

CPSIA compliance information: Batch #CW14GS: For further information contact Gareth Stevens, New York, New York at 1-800-542-2595.

CONTENTS

CRAFTY RECYCLING

You don't have to go shopping to fill your home with cool new decorations and handy objects. You can transform unwanted old stuff into all kinds of amazing craft items! All you need is a little imagination.

Going Global

Always remember to "reduce, reuse, and recycle." By turning old things into useful craft objects, you will be keeping them from going to landfill and helping our planet!

What a Load of Rubbish!

Your home is sure to be full of unwanted objects that could be used in craft projects. Plastic containers are always handy. Scrap paper can be used in many different ways. You could cut up old clothes for textile crafts. Your friends and family will be amazed when you tell them your new craft projects are mostly made from "junk"!

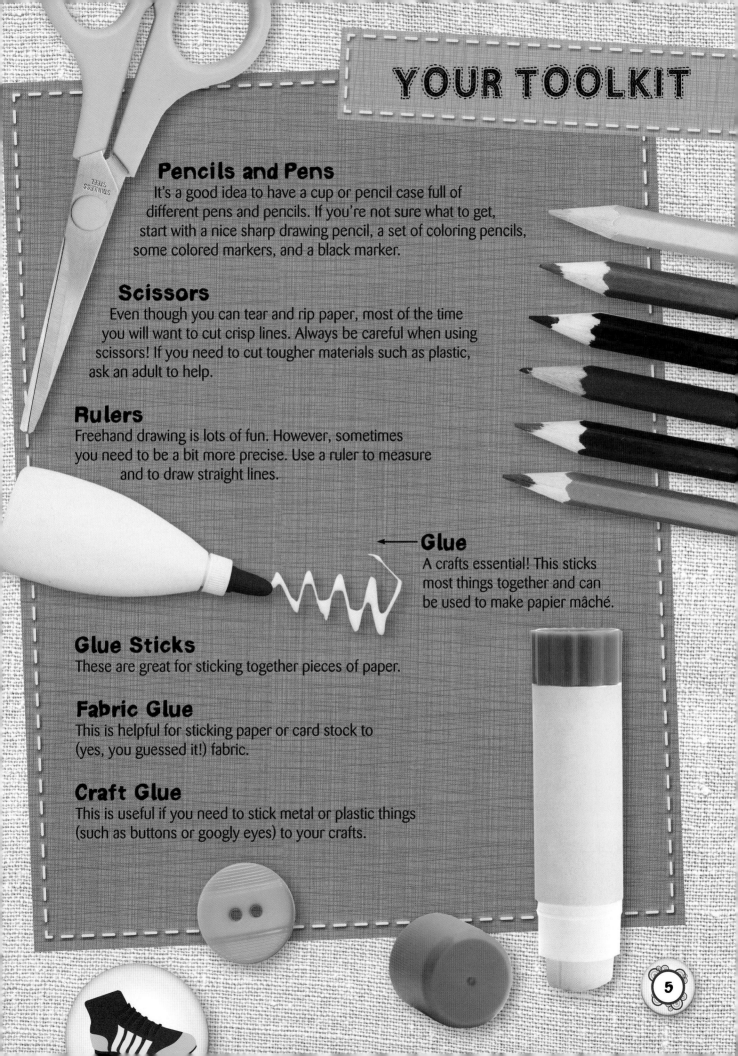

Pencils and Pens

It's a good idea to have a cup or pencil case full of different pens and pencils. If you're not sure what to get, start with a nice sharp drawing pencil, a set of coloring pencils, some colored markers, and a black marker.

Scissors

Even though you can tear and rip paper, most of the time you will want to cut crisp lines. Always be careful when using scissors! If you need to cut tougher materials such as plastic, ask an adult to help.

Rulers

Freehand drawing is lots of fun. However, sometimes you need to be a bit more precise. Use a ruler to measure and to draw straight lines.

Glue

A crafts essential! This sticks most things together and can be used to make papier mâché.

Glue Sticks

These are great for sticking together pieces of paper.

Fabric Glue

This is helpful for sticking paper or card stock to (yes, you guessed it!) fabric.

Craft Glue

This is useful if you need to stick metal or plastic things (such as buttons or googly eyes) to your crafts.

JAM JAR LANTERNS

You can easily turn jam jars into beautiful lanterns. They will brighten up any garden, or make a room feel really cozy. The more you make, the better they will look when it gets dark!

You will need

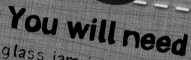

glass jam jar
tissue paper
wire
wire cutters
buttons
glue and brush
tea light and matches

1 Make sure your jam jar is clean. Coat the outside of the jar with a layer of glue.

2 Tear up your tissue paper into small pieces, and cover the outside of the jam jar with a layer of tissue paper in a single color.

3 Cut out leaf shapes from your tissue paper, using scissors. Choose colors that will stand out from your base layer.

4 Coat your jam jar with a layer of glue. Stick the tissue shapes on top. Then coat the whole jar with another layer of glue and let it dry.

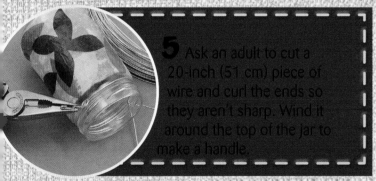

5 Ask an adult to cut a 20-inch (51 cm) piece of wire and curl the ends so they aren't sharp. Wind it around the top of the jar to make a handle.

6 You will need adult help for this step, too. Cut a 6-inch (15 cm) piece of wire and thread a few buttons onto it. Attach it to the wire handle and twist the ends again. Finally, put a tea light into the jar and light it.

BOTTLE TOPS IN BLOOM

This fun project will turn plastic bottle tops into flowers that you can use to decorate your room. The best part is that you don't need to water them to keep them looking pretty!

You will need
- bottle tops
- craft glue
- garden canes
- paper
- pen
- scissors
- sheets of colored foam
- vase or plastic bottle

1 Draw a petal shape onto a piece of paper with a pen. Cut it out to make a template.

2 Trace your template onto sheets of different colored foam. Cut out the petals. You will need five petals for each flower.

3 Trace your bottle top onto the foam twice, and cut it out. You will need two circles for each flower you make.

4 Glue your petals onto the flat part of the bottle top and leave them to dry.

5 Place a garden cane onto the back of the flower, and cover it with one of the foam circles, gluing it in place with the craft glue. Turn the flower over and cover the bottle cap with the other foam circle, gluing it down with the craft glue. Repeat steps 3 to 5 to make more flowers. Leave them to dry, then arrange them in a vase or plastic bottle.

FUNNY FACE VASE

Stop: don't throw away that empty milk jug! Save it from the trash and make this funky vase. When you put flowers in it, it will look like your crazy character has wild hair.

You will need

plastic milk jug
tissue paper and card stock
colored paper
glue
tape
acrylic paint
scissors
paintbrush

1 Ask an adult to help you cut the top off a plastic milk jug with a pair of scissors.

2 Draw two small circles (for nostrils), two medium-sized circles (for eyes), and a large circle (for ears) on the card stock. Cut them out with scissors. Then cut the large circle in half.

3 Stick the shapes to your bottle with tape, making the handle the nose.

4 Tear small pieces of tissue paper and stick them to the bottle with glue. This is called papier mâché! Keep going until the whole jug has been covered with paper and glue. Then leave it to dry.

5 Paint it all in a bright color using acrylic paint.

6 Cut out pieces of colored paper to add details to your funny face. Give it eyes, lips, and teeth. Glue them on, then leave it to dry before you start using it as a vase.

STACKABLE ROCKET BOXES

These space-themed boxes are made from empty food containers. You can use them to store little objects or hide secret stuff!

You will need

- cardboard packaging tubes with lids
- pencil
- colored paper
- glue stick
- tape
- scissors and ruler
- black marker

1 Find four tube-shaped containers that will fit neatly inside each other.

2 Measure the height of each tube, and cut a piece of paper to that height. Wrap paper around the tubes and tape it in place.

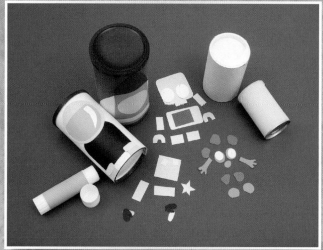

3 Draw the shapes that make up a rocket, an astronaut, a robot, and a spotty space alien onto colored paper. Cut out the paper shapes with scissors.

4 Glue all the paper shapes onto your containers with a glue stick.

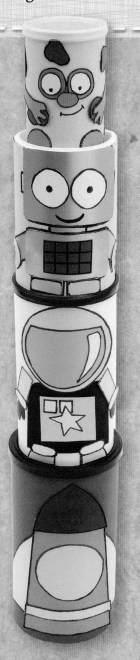

5 Outline the decorations with a black marker to add some detailing.

Your stackable containers don't need to have a space theme. They can be anything you want them to be.

13

BEACH HUT PEN CUPS

Spending time at the beach is a great thing to do in the summer. With this craft you can still be reminded of those sunny days even when it starts to rain.

You will need

2 paper towel tubes
cardboard
patterned paper
colored card stock
sandpaper
black marker
glue
scissors and ruler

1 Cut a piece of cardboard that measures 2.5 x 8 inches (6 x 20 cm).

2 Cut some sandpaper to the same size as your cardboard. Use glue to stick it to the cardboard.

3 Cut each paper towel tube in half, to make four tubes. Measure their height and cut four pieces of patterned paper to that height. Wrap the patterned paper around the tubes. Then, stick it in place with glue.

4 Cut out four rectangles of card stock measuring 3 x 1 inches (8 x 3 cm). Fold them down the middle, and cut a small notch into that fold. Then fold the edge of the card stock to the same depth as the notch. Cut four smaller 3 x 2-inch (8 x 6 cm) rectangles. Draw on a dot.

5 Glue the card stock shapes to your tubes with glue, as shown above. The pointed shapes are roofs, and the rectangles are doors. Glue the beach huts in a row on top of your sandpaper. Leave everything to dry.

BEDROOM PINBOARD

Are you always losing little notes, photos and cards? Then what you need is a personalized pinboard, to keep them all in one place! It's simple to make but looks great.

You will need

cardboard and paper
marker or pencil
fabric
ribbon and buttons
fabric glue
large plate
scissors

1 Trace the large plate onto your cardboard. Then cut out the circle.

2 Cover the cardboard circle with some fabric. Cut the fabric into a circle a little larger than the plate. Fold over the edge of the fabric, and stick it down with fabric glue.

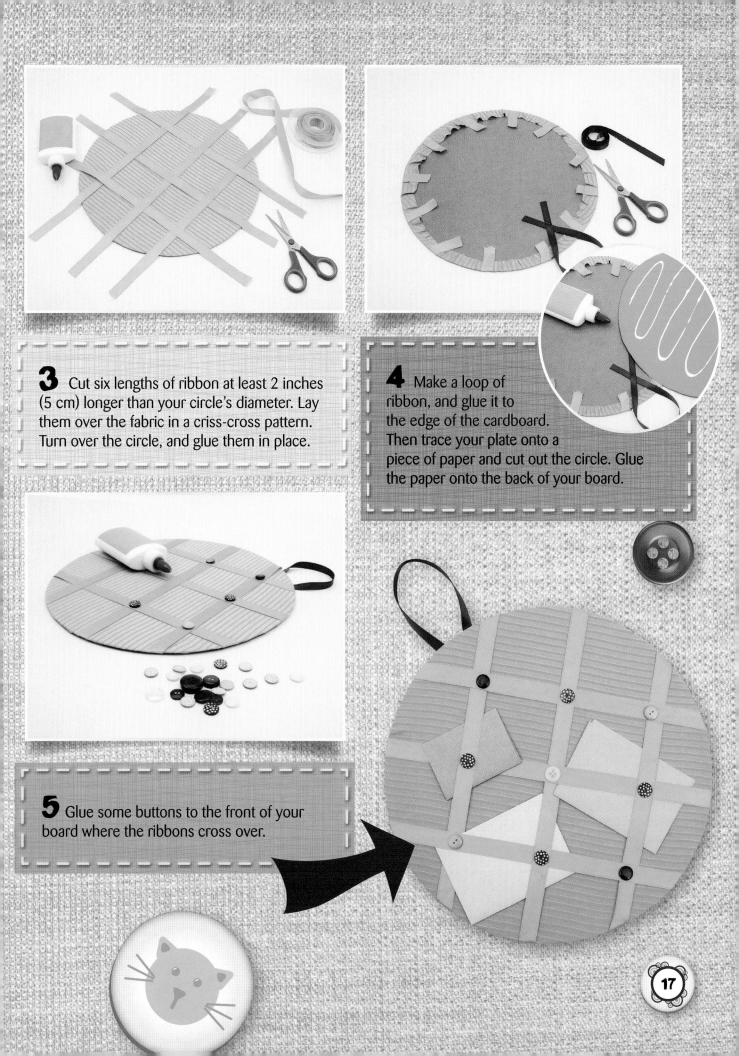

3 Cut six lengths of ribbon at least 2 inches (5 cm) longer than your circle's diameter. Lay them over the fabric in a criss-cross pattern. Turn over the circle, and glue them in place.

4 Make a loop of ribbon, and glue it to the edge of the cardboard. Then trace your plate onto a piece of paper and cut out the circle. Glue the paper onto the back of your board.

5 Glue some buttons to the front of your board where the ribbons cross over.

WATER BOTTLE BRACELETS

You wouldn't want to wear jewelry made of junk, right? Wrong! Here is how you can make a great bracelet from an old plastic bottle. It turns trash to treasure!

You will need

a 2-liter plastic bottle
yarn
metallic embroidery thread
tape
scissors
black marker
ruler

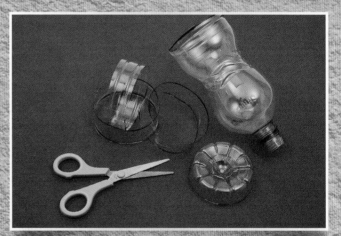

1 Draw lines around a plastic bottle with a marker. Use a ruler to measure them. They should be about 1 inch (2.5 cm) apart.

2 Cut along the lines to make plastic rings. These will be your bracelets!

3 Tape over the edges of each bracelet with some tape, so they are not sharp.

4 Wrap yarn around each plastic bracelet. Change colors to make stripes. When you're done, tie a knot.

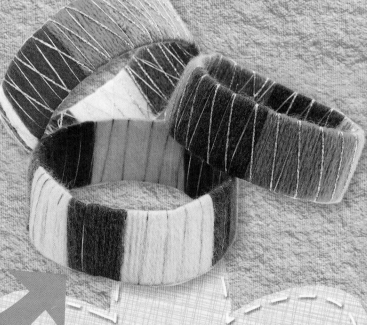

5 As a finishing touch, wind some metallic embroidery thread around each bracelet in a zig-zag.

You could also make some smaller rings from a smaller plastic bottle and attach them to a necklace or earrings!

SCRAP PAPER DAISY CHAIN

Rescue some paper from the trash or recycling bin, and you can make a daisy chain that lasts forever! If you don't have a paper shredder, just use scissors.

You will need
paper shredder or scissors,
ruler and pen
scrap paper
glue
green string
or yarn

1 Either shred some white and yellow paper, or use a ruler, pen, and scissors to cut it into long, straight strips. You will need 10 strips of yellow paper and 60 strips of white paper.

2 Coil the yellow paper into tight rings. Fix the ends in place with some glue. These rings will be the centers of your daisies.

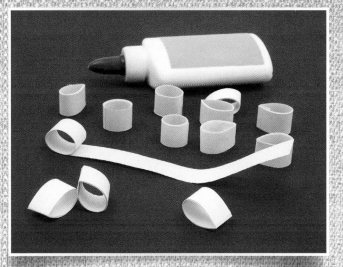

3 Now coil up the white paper into slightly larger rings. Fix the ends in place with some glue. Pinch one end of each white ring to make a point. These will make your petals.

4 Glue six white petals to each yellow ring. Leave them to dry on a protected surface.

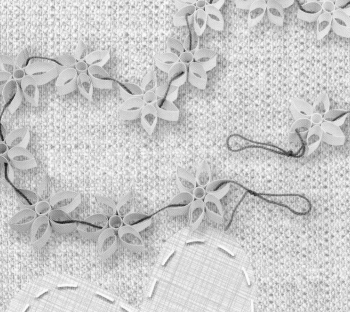

5 Thread the flowers onto a length of green string or yarn.

Make lots of different colored flowers using shredded magazines. You can use them to decorate picture frames, blank cards, or even a keepsake box.

PEACOCK BOOKENDS

If you enjoy making these peacocks, you could also try decorating bookends as lighthouses, rockets, or the turrets of a castle.

You'll be as proud as a peacock when you show everyone this fun craft. You can use these bird-brained buddies to prop up your books, or as a decoration.

1 Fill two chip cans with sand to make them heavy. Replace the lids and fix them in place with tape.

2 Measure the height of your cans. Cut two pieces of blue card stock to that height. Wrap them around the cans and tape them in place with double-sided tape.

3 Draw two body shapes like pinched ovals onto light blue card stock, and triangular beaks onto yellow card stock. Cut them out and stick them to the cans with double-sided tape. Then, stick on googly eyes with glue.

4 Cut out feather shapes from green, blue, and purple card stock. Stick the feathers to your can in a fan shape.

5 Add detail to your peacocks' bodies and feathers with markers and glitter glue.

23

SUNNY DAYS CLOCK

You should always make time for crafts... and now you can use crafts to make a timepiece! The rays of this cheery sunburst clock are made from scrap paper—or you could use newspaper.

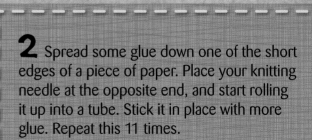

You will need

- a clock kit (from a craft store)
- scrap paper
- knitting needles
- pencil and paintbrush
- glue
- cardboard
- acrylic paint
- colored card stock
- scissors
- large cup

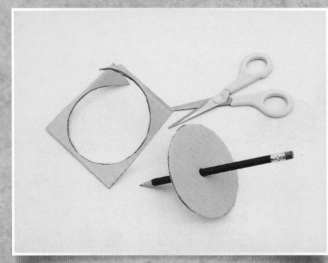

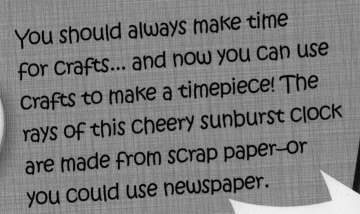

1 Trace a large cup onto cardboard. Make a hole in the middle with a pencil so that your clock pieces can fit through.

2 Spread some glue down one of the short edges of a piece of paper. Place your knitting needle at the opposite end, and start rolling it up into a tube. Stick it in place with more glue. Repeat this 11 times.

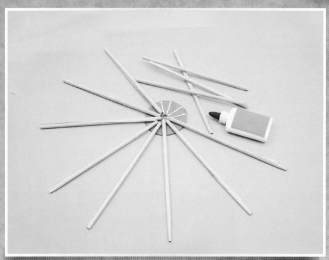

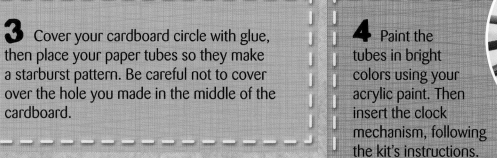

3 Cover your cardboard circle with glue, then place your paper tubes so they make a starburst pattern. Be careful not to cover over the hole you made in the middle of the cardboard.

4 Paint the tubes in bright colors using your acrylic paint. Then insert the clock mechanism, following the kit's instructions.

5 Cut out triangle shapes from colored card stock, and stick one on the end of each paper tube.

STARRY SKY MAIL MOBILE

Everyone loves receiving letters, but we usually just put the envelopes in the trash. Why not use them to make a fun mobile? Ask an adult to help with the last two steps.

1 Cut your envelopes into long strips, about 1 inch (3 cm) wide. Tie a knot in each strip.

2 Flatten each knot to make a pentagon shape. Wrap the rest of the paper strip around the pentagon and tuck the end into one of the folds.

3 Press in on the sides of a paper pentagon with your fingers, and push them in a little. This will push out the center of the shape, turning the flat pentagon into a 3-D star. Make about 40 to 50 stars. Paint some of them with acrylic paint.

4 Ask an adult to make a spiral out of wire. Thread the beads onto the wire and curl in either end of the wire to make sure the beads don't slide off.

5 You will need some more adult help with this step. Thread a needle, and push it through five stars in a row to link them together. Tie a knot at the end of the thread and cut it off with scissors. Make at least six starry chains, and tie them to the wire. Then add a loop of thread to the center of the spiral for hanging it up.

CD CASE PHOTO FRAME

Most people have some old, unwanted CDs at home. Don't throw them out just yet! You can use the cases to make snazzy photo frames!

1 Take apart your CD case, and turn around the front. Then clip it back together.

2 Measure, draw, and cut out a card stock frame the same size as your CD case. It should be 0.8 inch (2 cm) wide around the rim.

3 Cut some strips of felt about 0.4 inch (1 cm) wide and 10 inches (26 cm) long. You will need about 36 strips in different colors.

4 Put two different colored strips of felt together, and roll them up. Glue the ends down so that the coil doesn't unravel.

5 Glue the felt coils to the card stock, and leave to dry. Then glue the card stock onto the CD case on three sides. Leave one side open so you can insert a photograph.

PLASTIC BAG WEAVING

Every household seems to have a drawer or cupboard bursting with plastic bags! By weaving several bags together, you can make this cute, colorful pencil case.

You will need
plastic bags
tape
cardboard
scissors
ruler

1 Cut a piece of cardboard into a rectangle that measures 4 x 8 inches (10 x 20 cm). Snip five small triangles into each of the short sides.

2 Cut the plastic bags into 0.4-inch (1 cm) wide pieces, so you have strips ready to weave with.

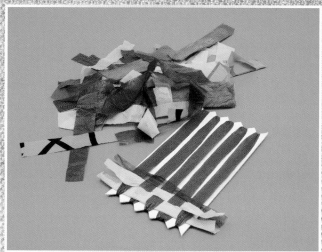

3 Wind strips around the grooves in the card stock so that you make lines of color. Stick them in place with tape.

4 Use different colored strips of plastic bag to weave in and out of the longer pieces. You will end up with a colorful checkerboard effect.

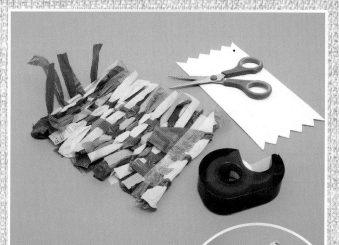

5 Cut the weaving off the board, making sure it doesn't unravel. Fold over the loose edges to make a rectangle and fix it in place with your tape. Repeat steps 2 through 5 so that you have two woven rectangles. Use more tape to attach the two pieces together on three sides. This will make your handy pencil case.

You could also make a pouch for your cell phone or music player. Just change the size of the cardboard in step 1 to make the case smaller.

GLOSSARY

container An object designed for storing or transporting one or more other objects.

freehand Drawn by hand, without using guiding tools such as rulers.

landfill A place where waste is disposed of by burying.

papier mâché A hard material made by layering paper and glue.

tea light A small candle in a metal case.

template An object that can be copied.

turret A small tower attached to a larger tower.

FURTHER READING

The Art of Recycling by Laura C. Martin (Storey Books, 2004)

Eco-Friendly Crafting with Kids by Kate Lilley (Ryland, Peters and Small, 2012)

Green Crafts for Children by Emma Hardy (CICO Books, 2011)

What Shall We Do Today? by Catherine Woram (Ryland, Peters and Small, 2009)

WEBSITES

kids.nationalgeographic.co.uk/kids/activities/crafts/
Crafts inspired by nature.

www.freekidscrafts.com/recycled_crafts-t27.html
Lots of ideas for recycled crafts.

www.kinderart.com/index.html
Art projects categorized by theme and age.

INDEX